SPIDER GETS A BOW

Donna Guran

Illustrated by: Natalie Birholtz
natalie.birholtz01@gmail.com
nataliebirholtzart.square space.com
Instagram @natbirholtz_art_

Library of Congress Control Number: 2018675309
Printed in the United States of America

For River Aiden

Halloween had come and gone.
All the candy had been eaten!

The decorations were put away—the witches and skeletons, the ghosts and goblins, even the pumpkins were back in their boxes.

Still, Spider hung above the front door.

"Hugo, it's time for Spider to come down."

"Guess what, Mama. Spiders have eight legs," said Hugo.

"Yes," said Mama, "spiders have eight legs."

"Mom! Mom! Mama! Guess what, Mama."

"What?" She asked.

"Spiders have eight eyes."

"Yes, that's true, spiders do have eight eyes. But Thanksgiving will be here soon. Why don't we hang up that turkey you drew?"

"Ok, Spider can watch!" said Hugo.

Mama found the tape and together they hung the
turkey in the window.

"There, we're almost ready for Thanksgiving. Let's put Spider away until next year," Mama said.

"Please, can't Spider stay a little longer?" Hugo asked.

Mama laughed. "Well, ok, maybe just a little longer. Bedtime now."

Hugo went to the door and looked up at Spider.
"Guess what, Spider. You can stay! Goodnight now," Hugo
whispered
Spider's eight eyes looked down at Hugo.

"Guess what, Mama. I think Spider winked at me!"

Mama smiled.

Thanksgiving Day arrived, and Mama made a big dinner.

Hugo made swimming pools out of mashed potatoes. He pretended that his broccoli was a tree.

"Mama, do you think Spider would like the rest of my turkey?"

"Probably not," she said.

"Sweet potatoes?"

"I don't think so."

"Stuffing?"

"Stuffing is for little boys, not for spiders," Mama said.

"I'm just teasing you, Mama! Spiders eat insects!" Hugo laughed. "I never ate an insect!"

"And I hope you never do!" said Mama.

The very next day, Mama and Hugo took the turkey picture down from the window.

"Are you ready to put Spider away?" Mama asked.

"I think Spider should stay."

Mama was surprised. "Even through Christmas?"

"Yes PLEEEEEEEASE let Spider stay until Christmas, Mama!! I don't want him to go away."

"Well, I guess I *am* getting used to seeing him up there."
"Me too," said Hugo.

"I suppose he can stay while we decorate."

Hugo helped Mama bake cookies.

Then they put the ornaments on the tree. Mama hung the lights.

"The star goes on top, doesn't it?" Hugo asked.

"That's right," Mama said.

Hugo was quiet for a minute, thinking.

"Guess what, Mama."

"What?"

"Spider wants a decoration, too."

"Well, I think I have just the thing," Mama said.

She reached into a box and pulled out a big red bow.

"What do you think of this?" she asked. Hugo clapped his hands together and said, "He's gonna look great!"

"Ok, let's see how he likes it," she said, and she placed the bow on Spider's back.

"Well?"

"Guess what, Mama. He loves it!" Hugo said.

And so Spider got to stay. At least until Christmas.